WELCOME TO THE CONSTRUCTION SITE

Concrete Mixer

1

Samantha Bell

Published in the United States of America
by Cherry Lake Publishing
Ann Arbor, Michigan
www.cherrylakepublishing.com

Content Adviser: Louis Teel, Professor of Heavy Equipment Operating,
Central Arizona College
Reading Adviser: Cecilia Minden, PhD, Literacy expert and children's author

Photo Credits: ©lumen-digital / Shutterstock, cover, 2; ©wanphen
chawarung / Shutterstock, 4; ©Monkey Business Images / Shutterstock, 6;
©Blanscape / Shutterstock, 8; ©Dr Ajay Kumar Singh / Shutterstock, 10;
©AstroStar / Shutterstock, 12; ©alexfan32 / Shutterstock, 14; ©Henk Jacobs /
Shutterstock, 16; ©Alison Hancock / Shutterstock, 18; ©Avtolik /
Shutterstock, 20

Library of Congress Cataloging-in-Publication Data has been filed and is
available at catalog.loc.gov

Cherry Lake Publishing would like to acknowledge the work of The Partnership
for 21st Century Learning. Please visit www.p21.org for more information.

Printed in the United States of America
Corporate Graphics

Table of Contents

Hard and Strong

Concrete mixers mix concrete for building. Concrete is hard and strong.

**What do workers wear
to stay safe?**

Some mixers are small. They are used for small jobs.

Some mixers are on trucks. They are used for big jobs.

How do the blades help?

Most mixers have a **drum**. The drum has **blades** inside.

Mixing It Up

Workers put **cement** into the drum. They add other things like **gravel** and sand. Then they add water.

A machine turns the drum. The blades mix everything together. It becomes concrete.

Pouring Concrete

A **chute** is attached to the drum.

The concrete goes down the chute. It is poured where it is needed. It quickly becomes hard.

Back to Work

Workers clean the mixer. It is ready to make more concrete!

Find Out More

Book

Lennie, Charles. *Concrete Mixers*. Minneapolis: ABDO Kids, 2015.

Website

Ten Random Facts—Cement Truck
www.tenrandomfacts.com/cement-truck/
Find out more about cement trucks at this site.

Glossary

blades (BLADEZ) the flat, sharp-edged parts of tools

cement (suh-MENT) a gray powder made from a crushed rock called limestone that is used to make concrete

chute (SHOOT) a narrow pathway that sends things down to a lower level

concrete (KAHN-kreet) something needed for building, made by mixing sand, gravel, cement, and water together

drum (DRUHM) the large main part of a concrete mixer that holds the concrete

gravel (GRAV-uhl) small pieces of rock

Home and School Connection

Use this list of words from the book to help your child become a better reader. Word games and writing activities can help beginning readers reinforce literacy skills.

a	everything	mixer	the
add	for	mixers	then
and	goes	more	they
are	gravel	needed	things
attached	hard	on	to
becomes	has	other	together
big	have	poured	trucks
blades	inside	put	turns
building	into	quickly	used
cement	is	ready	water
chute	it	safe	where
clean	jobs	sand	
concrete	like	small	
down	make	stay	
drum	mix	strong	

Index

About the Author

Samantha Bell has written and illustrated over 60 books for children. She lives in South Carolina with her family and pets.